DELTA PUBLISHING

PICTURE PROMPTS
Adjectives

Susan Thomas

Miniflashcards
Language Games

Picture Prompts: Adjectives

CONTENTS

- **Section 1**   3
  Introduction
  1.1   What Picture Prompts contains
  1.2   Using games in the language classroom
  1.3   Preparing the picture sheets
  1.4   Using the picture sheets
  1.5   Language presentation
  1.6   Practice activities and games
         1.6.1   Varying the activities
  1.7   Assessment
         1.7.1   Self-assessment
         1.7.2   Teacher assessment
  1.8   Grammar Practice
         1.8.1   Adjectives
         1.8.2   Prepositions and Directions
  1.9   Using spinners
  1.10   Using game boards

- **Section 2**   6
  Using the pictures
  2.1   Use in class
  2.2   Using the OHP: why
  2.3   Using the OHP: how

- **Section 3**   7
  Standard games and activities

- **Lesson notes**   12

- **Spinners**   44

- **Game boards**   46

- **Language Chart**   48

First published 1997

© DELTA Publishing 1997
© Artwork and original text MiniFlashcard Language Games 1996

Typesetting by CjB Editorial Plus

Text and cover design by Darren Watts

Printed and bound in the UK

Project Management: Swan Communication Ltd, England
Adapted Text: Susan Holden

All rights reserved. No reproduction, copy or transmission of this publication may be made without written permission, except that the picture sets may be photocopied as indicated for non-commercial purposes.
Based on material developed by MiniFlashcard Language Games, PO Box 1526, London W7 1ND.

This edition published by DELTA Publishing, 39 Alexandra Road, Addlestone, Surrey KT15 2PQ.

ISBN: 1 900783 16 9

SECTION 1

Introduction to *Picture Prompts*

1.1 What *Picture Prompts* contains

Notes

Each *Picture Prompts* book contains:
- a description of ways of using games and game-like activities in foreign language teaching;
- a menu of 20–30 standard activities which can be used with the specific picture cards;
- photocopiable sets of pictures to use around a theme (eg Clothes), or to provide practice in a specific language area (eg Phrasal Verbs or Adjectives);
- instructions for using the pictures, including:
  – vocabulary list;
  – useful language;
  – suitable standard activities;
  – additional activities;
- spinners to photocopy and cut out for use with games;
- blank boards to photocopy and use to make your own games.

Each book thus provides a rich resource of ideas and photocopiable materials which can be used with a wide range of age groups and language levels.

1.2 Using games in the language classroom

Notes

Games and game-like activities provide excellent ways of allowing learners to practise language in a relaxed, creative way. They encourage the repetition of key language items in a way which is motivating and challenging. New lexical items and grammatical structures can be used within familiar game-like formats, thus providing the slower learners with support and guidance, while allowing the faster ones to use their creativity.

The practice provided through *Picture Prompts* extends that contained in the course book, and allows mixed ability classes to work in groups at their own pace.

1.3 Preparing the picture sheets

Notes

The picture sheets can be prepared in different ways:
- They can be photocopied onto paper, for use as handouts or worksheets.
- They can be enlarged, for use as flashcards or posters.
- They can be copied onto card, and cut out, to make individual cards for use in games.
- Text can be added beneath the pictures, or on the back.
- To protect the pictures, they can be copied onto paper, glued onto card, and then covered with acetate.
- They can be photocopied onto acetate to provide OHP transparencies.
- The visuals can be combined or grouped to make display materials, or to make a picture dictionary or topic reference book.
- The blank masters can be used to create new sets of visuals, and to make matching text cards and new games.

1.4 Using the picture sheets

Notes

The visuals can be used to:
- introduce a new word or phrase;
- serve as a prompt for spoken language in a practice or review activity;
- serve as a reminder of the meaning of a written word or phrase;
- provide the starting point for introducing or revising related vocabulary;
- illustrate a structure, often in combination with other pictures;
- provide a series of examples to illustrate a teaching point;
- provide random prompts, when used in conjunction with a spinner or die, for practice or assessment.

1.5 Language presentation

Notes

Introduce new language, using the visuals as flashcards, or on the OHP. Provide plenty of time for the language to be heard and practised before you ask any student to speak alone. Chorus work and class repetition are useful here. Encourage the learners to experiment with their voices: they can repeat the words in different ways, eg emphatically, softly, angrily, questioningly, etc. This helps to avoid boredom, and encourages good intonation and pronunciation.

Learners who are good at relating sounds and visuals will find that they can easily associate language items with the illustrations. Others may find it useful to see the written form as well, so introduction of this should not be delayed. At this stage, attention should be drawn to differences between pronunciation of the written form in English and the students' own language. In this way, these items can be used later as production models by the students.

1.6 Practice activities and games

Notes

Once the learners are familiar with the new vocabulary items, individual or group activities and games can be set up to practise them. Such activities will provide opportunities to practise the items in context, and in association with specific language structures and functions. This will help them transfer the language into their long-term memories.

During the course of an activity, you should help the students with any lexical items or pronunciation features which they are unsure of.

Section 3 (page 7) sets out a collection of standard activity-types which can be used with any of the picture sheets in this book.

The language notes opposite each page of pictures give activities which are designed specifically for that visual set.

1.6.1 Varying the activities

Most of the standard activities are based on well-known games and may be familiar to your class. Younger learners are often very good at making up their own variations, while older ones may rely on you to suggest these. However, adults usually respond well, as they can practise actively without using the language 'in public'.

The important thing is that the learners are practising the language in an active, meaningful way, and are also having fun. Some of the games may generate noise; others are quite quiet. Some are competitive; others require co-operation.

You may wish to decide how to encourage weaker students in the competitive games. These can often be made into exciting team events, using mixed ability teams, with a time element. If this involves physical movement, make sure there are no hazards in the classroom!

For extended practice, you may wish to get the students to move round the room after each game, changing partners and groups. Most games last between 5 and 15 minutes, although the writing activities generally take longer.

Allow time at the end of a game to discuss difficulties, and ideas for varying or improving the game. There may be ways of adapting it to reflect the students' own interests more closely.

1.7 Assessment

Notes

1.7.1 Self-assessment

Activities and games based on picture cards are ideal for encouraging the learners to assess their own progress. Once they are sure of particular language items, they can discard these particular cards and use more unfamiliar ones. The cards can be used together later for a test.

1.7.2 Teacher assessment

This can take place:
- during a teacher-controlled activity with the OHP;
- by observing individuals and pairs at work;
- by joining in with groups or individuals during an activity;
- by providing individuals or groups with a worksheet, based on the same visuals.

Such feedback provides information for future reteaching, or for planning future work.

1.8 Grammar practice

Notes

Collections of Picture Prompts such as those in the *Adjectives*, and the *Prepositions and Directions* books, can also be used to practise specific grammar patterns, as well as for general communication activities.

1.8.1 Adjectives

The pictures can be used to practise the:
- order of adjectives when more than one is used to describe a noun;
- formation of comparatives and superlatives;
- relationship between adjectives and adverbs.

1.8.2 Prepositions and Directions

The pictures in this book can be used to practise:
- difference in choice of prepositions between L1 and English;
- use of preposition and article.

1.9 Using spinners

Notes

Language spinners or dice can be used in connection with the picture sets.
The photocopiable spinners included in this book are:
- colour (x 2)
- mood
- twenty-sided numbered spinner.

In addition, there are blank spinners for you to create your own versions.

How to prepare
Photocopy the spinners onto thin card, or photocopy onto paper and stick this onto thicker card. Make a hole in the middle, and push a long match-stick, or a toothpick, through the hole. Secure this with scotch tape or blutak.

1.10 Using game boards

Notes

Two photocopiable game boards are provided, one with twelve squares and one with twenty squares.

These can be used to adapt the existing picture sets, or to make new games.

SECTION 2

Using the Pictures

The pictures contained in this book can be used singly, or in a variety of combinations, to support work at different stages of the language programme. They can also be used with students of different abilities, needs and ages.

2.1 Use in class

Notes

The visuals can be used:
- with the whole class, to introduce vocabulary and concepts;
- with individual students and groups, to practise or revise specific language items.

They can be:
- combined in many different ways to illustrate relationships between different areas of vocabulary;
- used in random groups to introduce variety and an element of challenge;
- introduced singly or in groups as the starting point for using language creatively.

Board games (page 46) involving the visuals and/or dice and spinners, can be used to set up group activities which are simple or demanding.

2.2 Using the OHP: why

Notes

If available, an OHP is particularly useful for introducing new vocabulary. It can also be used for whole-class work at various stages in the language programme. It can be used to:
- ensure that the students understand the concepts underlying the activity;
- review previously-taught language items before introducing new, associated vocabulary;
- present new language;
- provide teacher-led practice of new language;
- assess whether the new language has been well enough learned for the students to go on to group work activities;
- play whole-class games;
- demonstrate the rules of a game before it is played in groups;
- invite suggestions from the students on ways of using language items in different situations;
- encourage activities which require the students to make creative use of the language they have learned;
- organise feedback on an activity;
- assess learning;
- revise items which were learned earlier in the programme.

2.3 Using the OHP: how

Notes

There are many ways of using the pictures on the OHP. Here are several, which will add variety and interest to your lesson.

- Move the pictures slowly into focus and ask the students to name them.
- Flash the picture up. If it is not named, repeat more slowly.
- Reveal sections of the picture bit by bit.
- Cut the picture into sections, and put on the OHP in random order, and/or upside down. Ask the students to reassemble in the correct order.
- Use as silhouettes.
- Use a keyhole shape cut out of card as a frame. Play 'Through the Keyhole' guessing games.
- Colour the pictures using instructions from the class.
- Add overlays for items such as the price of clothes.
- Use for whole-class games such as *Noughts and Crosses* [3]; *What's on the Card?* [1]; *Kim's Game* [6]; *True or False?* [14]; and *Guessing Game* [13].

SECTION 3

Standard Games and Activities

The first group of 18 games and activities described here can be used with any sheet of Picture Prompts in any book of the series, although you may want to vary them slightly. Each is cross-referenced by a number, eg [1], in the individual Lesson Notes.

The second group (page 11) can be used with any sheet of Picture Prompts in this book.

[1]
What's on the Card? — memorising; consolidating

- **Equipment:** 20+ picture cards with text on the back, or a checklist of the text.

a Picture Spread — free choice of visible cards

Spread the cards face up on a table. Take it in turns to pick a card and name it. If you are right, keep the card. If you are wrong, put it back. The player with most cards at the end is the winner.

b Pick a Card — free choice of unseen cards

One player fans out the cards, face down. One player chooses a card and tries to name it. If correct, you keep the card. If incorrect, you put it back, and the cards are shuffled before the next player chooses. The winner is the player with most cards at the end,

c Take that Card — no choice of card

Place the pile of cards on the table, face up. Take it in turns to name the top card, If you are correct, you keep it. If you are incorrect, that card goes to the bottom of the pile. Winner as before.

Variation: If you do not know a card, put it face up on the table in front of you.
It becomes a penalty card. At the end of the game, take it in turns to name these cards. Whoever names the card correctly, wins it.

d Guess the Card — choice of unseen cards

Place a number of cards on the table, face down (no text on back). Take it in turns to choose and name a card. If you are correct: keep it. If you are incorrect: put it back. Winner as before.

e Quick Flash — no choice of card; time pressure

One person holds up a card for one second only. The first player to name it correctly keeps it. Winner as before.

[2]
Line Solitaire — memorising; consolidating; revising

- **Equipment:** 10+ cards per player.

Basic version — individual learning

Lay out some cards in a line, face up. Name the first item, and then check with the word on the back. If you get it right, carry on. If you are wrong, learn the word. Then shuffle the cards, lay them out in a new line, and begin again. The winner is the player who completes the longest line.

Variation 1: Put the cards in a diamond or pyramid shape, or in rows of six, and see how many rows you can get right.

Variation 2: Lay the cards in a square 4x4 (you need 16 cards per player). Move from corner to corner in the smallest number of moves.

[3]
Noughts and Crosses   **consolidating; revising; monitoring**

● **Equipment:**   nine cards.

Basic version
Lay the cards face up in a 3x3 shape. Take it in turns to name them. If you are correct, turn the card over, or put a coloured counter on it. The next player tries to name a card next door to it. Three named cards in a row wins the game.

[4]
Three in a Row   **creative use of language**

● **Equipment:**   any page of 20 pictures relating to a topic. Three counters for each player.

Basic version
Choose a picture square, and name the item on it, or say something about the picture. If you are right, put a coloured counter on it. The first player with three counters in a row is the winner.

Variation: Use a 20-sided spinner. Proceed as above, but use the spinner to select the squares.

[5]
I Spy ...   **consolidating; revising**

● **Equipment:**   cards.

Basic version
Put some cards face up on the table. One player calls out the first letter of an item. The first player to point to a correct card beginning with that letter, wins it. That player calls the next letter. The winner is the player with most cards at the end of the game.

[6]
Kim's Game   **consolidating; revising**

● **Equipment:**   cards.

Basic version
Spread out cards face up on the table. All the players turn away, and one player removes one card. The first player to name the missing card wins a point.

[7]
Bingo   **consolidating; revising; listening**

● **Equipment:**   a sheet of 20 cards on a picture board for each player. Eight counters for each player.

Basic version
Each player chooses eight items from the 20-picture sheet and puts a cross in the corner of each. The quiz person calls out the 20 items in any order. If you have put a cross next to that item, you can put a counter on it. The first player to put a counter on all their marked squares calls 'Bingo!' and is the winner.

Variation 1: The quiz person uses the 20-sided spinner to select the words called.

Variation 2: Spread out 20 cards face up on the table. The quiz person removes them, and you write down ten words you can remember. The quiz person then shuffles the cards, and puts them down one after the other. Check your ten words against these. The first player to have ten words correctly spelled on their list is the winner.

[8]
Charades   consolidating; revising
● Equipment: cards.

Basic version
The first player chooses a card and mimes the item for the others to guess.

[9]
Snap   consolidating; revising
● Equipment: four sets of cards from the current topic, or previous ones.

Basic version
Shuffle the cards and deal them out. Each player takes it in turn to put a card face up on the table. If two similar cards are put down, the first player to name the cards correctly wins them.

[10]
Dominoes   consolidating; reading
● Equipment: sets of dominoes with pictures and text, using the blank square templates (page 56).

Basic version
Distribute six dominoes to each player. Put one domino in the centre of the table. Take it in turns to put your dominoes down, as you match words and pictures.

[11]
Matching Pairs   consolidating; revising
● Equipment: two sets of picture cards.

Basic version
Shuffle the cards and spread them out face down. The first player turns over two cards. If they are the same, and if you can name them correctly, you can keep them, and have another turn. If they do not match, or if you cannot name them, the cards are put back. It is then the next player's turn.

[12]
I Went to Market   consolidating; revising
● Equipment: cards.

Basic version
Spread suitable cards face up on the table. One player says "I went to market, and I bought ...", and adds an item using the cards on the table as a prompt. The next player repeats the sentence and adds another item.
>   "I went to the market and I bought (some shoes)."
>   "I went to the market and I bought (some shoes) and (a new jacket)."

Any player who gets the sentence wrong, or cannot name a new item, drops out.

[13]
Guessing Game   creative use of language
● Equipment: set of cards relating to current topic.

Basic version
The first player thinks of one of the cards and says something about it. The first person to identify the card, wins it.

[14]
True or False?   listening

● Equipment: a sheet of cards.

Basic version
One person points to a card, and makes a true or false statement about it. The person who correctly says "True" or "False" wins the card.

Variation 1: As above, but the second player repeats the sentence if it is true, or corrects it if it is false.

Variation 2: One person reads out a list of true or false statements about the pictures. The players make a note of whether each is true or false.

[15]
Battleship Buddies   speaking; listening

● Equipment: two identical sets of nine cards for each pair.

Basic version   **pairwork**
Player A puts the cards in a 3x3 shape behind a book, so that Player B cannot see them. Player A describes each card, and says where it is, eg "In the middle of the top row". Player B tries to arrange his/her cards in the same way. Then they compare.

Variation: Draw pictures on the grid, instead of using cards.

[16]
Following Instructions   listening

● Equipment: one identical picture for each student.

Basic version
Give instructions to follow, eg:

> "Draw a flower in the middle of the T-shirt. Give it some leaves. Colour the flower red and the T-shirt yellow. Then put a cross at the bottom of the picture. Now draw a line across the top of the picture. Finally, fold the picture into four, and put it in your coursebook between pages 60 and 61."

Ask the students to compare what they have done.

[17]
Spot the Difference   **creative use of language; speaking; listening**

● Equipment: two enlarged copies of a picture for each pair.

Basic version   **pairwork**
Player A changes his/her picture by adding or deleting things. Player B asks questions to find out what the changes are, and makes similar changes. Compare your pictures.

[18]
Storytime   **creative use of language; writing**

● Equipment: mixed cards.

Basic version
Give each player some cards from mixed sets. Each player has 10-15 minutes to write a short story, incorporating the items on these cards. Each person then reads out their story.

Variation 1: One player starts the story as an oral activity. The others take it in turns to add a sentence.

Variation 2: Use the activity for homework, and ask the students to record their stories on a cassette. Play them back in class.

Variation 3: Learners or groups select three or four cards at random. They then make up a story, or act out a scene, using the cards as prompts.

Standard activities which can be used with any sheet of Picture Prompts in this book.

[19]
Twenty Questions — **creative use of language; speaking; listening**

- **Equipment:** adjective pictures.

Basic version
Think of an object and choose adjectives which describe it. The other players try to guess your object. They can only ask "yes/no" type questions.

[20]
Story Time — **creative use of language; writing**

- **Equipment:** a selection of adjectives.

Basic version
Make up a story, using as many adjectives as possible.

[21]
Simon Says — **listening**

- **Equipment:** selected cards for each player.

Basic version — **pairwork**
One player gives instructions to move the cards, eg
"Put your pen on the table. Put the pencil next to the pen. Put the pen under your book ..."

| LESSON NOTES | **Colours and Colour Spinners (pages 44 and 45)** |

Colour spinners or colour cards are a useful way to teach and practise the colours, either alone or together with objects.

The spinners on pages 44 and 45 can be copied and coloured to provide this practice.

Key language

Notes

Adjective on its own
red, green, blue, yellow, purple, white
orange, pink, brown, grey, gold, black

Adjective + classroom objects (adjective + noun)
What colour is the book?   The book is /It's red.
This is a/the red book.   It's red.
Show me the blue book.
Is it a red pen or a green pen?   It's green.
The pens are red.   These are red pens.
These pens are red.   Those pens are green.

Adjective + holidays
blue sky   grey sky   blue sea   yellow sand   white hotel

Adjectives in combination (use two spinners, colour + number)
ten green bottles
two green eyes
four black cats

Adjectives + picture cards (adjective + noun)
a white T-shirt
He is wearing blue jeans.

Practising colours: activities

Notes

What is it?
Spin the spinner. The first player to say the colour where it stops is the winner.

Coloured cards
Make coloured cards for each of the twelve colours listed above.
Use them to play:
[2] Line Solitaire; [3] Noughts and Crosses; [5] I Spy ...; [6] Kim's Game
[14] True or False?

Matching Pairs with the Spinner and Picture Cards
Take it in turns to spin the spinner. When it stops, say the colour, and take a card of the same colour if you are correct. The player with most cards is the winner.

Practising colours as adjectives

Notes

Practise naming an item with its colour, using:
- classroom objects
- pupil's clothing
- the General Objects from page 39 coloured in
- magazine pictures

Also: spin the spinner and find an object of the same colour.

Additional activities

Notes

Odd one out
Ask the students to draw and colour pictures, and make statements:
  There are three brown dogs and one white dog. (adjective + noun)
  There are three large brown dogs and one small white dog. (adjective order + noun)

Classroom stickers
Write the names of colours on small cards. The students stick them on objects in the classroom. Encourage them to put them on different things in each lesson.

LESSON NOTES

Adjectives and their Opposites
(pages 13 to 16)

Key Language

1 round/square
2 rectangular/triangular
3 straight/curved
4 large/medium/small
5 long/short
6 thick/thin
7 narrow/wide
8 heavy/light
9 hard/soft
10 rough/smooth
11 light/dark
12 glass/plastic
13 wooden/metal
14 paper/made of material
15 fast/slow
16 loud/quiet
17 hot/cold
18 expensive/cheap
19 new/old
20 beautiful/ugly

21 comfortable/uncomfortable
22 wet/dry
23 clean/dirty
24 tidy/untidy
25 full/empty
26 deep/shallow
27 high/low
28 busy/quiet
29 shut/open
30 vacant/engaged
31 present/absent
32 delicious/awful
33 fun/boring
34 wonderful/terrible
35 dangerous/safe
36 same/different
37 easy/difficult
38 right/wrong
39 first/last
40 fair/unfair

Notes

Synonyms
large/big

Extremes
enormous   dirty
tiny   filthy

Opposites
big/small   cheap/expensive

Modifiers or intensifiers + adjective
quite
so   hot
very
dreadfully

Comparatives
	as big	
This house is	not as big	as that one.
	nearly as big	

Superlatives
The biggest room
This room is the biggest.

Modification of comparatives and superlatives
Much bigger   By far the biggest

The adjectives in this book include those of:

Notes

shape	dimension	weight	texture	colour
material	age	appearance	value	audibility
temperature	rapidity	moisture	accessibility	taste
quality	physical condition	similarity	correctness	

Standard games and activities (see Section 3 pages 7–11)

Notes		
	[2]	Line Solitaire
	[3]	Noughts and Crosses
	[5]	I Spy ...
	[6]	Kim's Game
	[4]	Three in a Row
	[8]	Charades
	[14]	True or False?

Choose a card and make a statement about the item and the adjective.

[13] Guessing Game
    a) Describe a picture without mentioning the adjective(s). The first player to guess them wins the card.
    b) Describe an object.
       It's green, made of plastic, and has pens in it. (Pencil case)

[19] Twenty Questions
One player thinks of an object. The others have twenty questions to guess it.
Is it made of paper?   Is it made of plastic?   Is it round?

[12] I Went to Market
... and bought a cheap watch, a cheap dress.   some cheap shoes ...

[11] Matching Pairs
Bring in magazine pictures of objects. Write adjectives to describe them on pieces of paper. The other players must match each adjective to the picture(s).

Additional activities

Notes

Odd one out

Ask the students to draw and colour pictures, and make statements:
There are three brown dogs and one white dog.   (adjective + noun)
There are three large brown dogs and one small white dog.   (adjective order + noun)

Classroom stickers

Write the names of colours on small cards. The students stick them on objects in the classroom. Encourage them to put them on different things in each lesson.

Think of something that ...

Put selected cards into piles, eg Pile A: 'made of'   Pile B: materials
Make sentences, taking a card from each pile.
    The book is made of paper.

Classification

Take it in turns to take a card, and name (five) objects which it can describe.
    (big)   table, door, curtain, poster, window

What's in the bag?

Put objects in a bag. Take it in turns to put your hand in the bag and describe an object. The others guess it.
    It's round...smooth...hard ...   (a stone)

Who's got what?

Ask the students to bring objects that are long/heavy/short/fat, etc. Ask them to compare them.
    Maria's pencil is longer than Paulo's. But Anna's is the longest.

Adjectives

Adjectives

| LESSON NOTES | # Adjectives on their own (pages 17 to 21) |

These pictures are similar to those on the Adjectives Opposites pages, but represent each adjective separately.

Useful language

Notes

As on page 13.

Additional language

Notes

The dog is big/small. The/A big/small dog.
This one/That one.
This dog is (big). That one is (small). This dog is the biggest.
This pool is deeper than that pool.

Standard games and activities (see Section 3 pages 7–11)

Notes

[2] Line Solitaire
[3] Noughts and Crosses
[5] I Spy ...
[6] Kim's Game
[4] Three in a Row
[8] Charades
[14] True or False?
Choose a card and make a statement about the item and the adjective.
[13] Guessing Game
a) Describe a picture without mentioning the adjective(s). The first player to guess them wins the card.
b) Describe an object.
It's green, made of plastic, and has pens in it. (Pencil case)
[19] Twenty Questions
One player thinks of an object. The others have twenty questions to guess it.
Is it made of paper? Is it made of plastic? Is it round?

Additional activities

Notes

Join the opposites

Each player writes out lists of opposite adjectives. Their partner tries to join these up without crossing another line:

round	hard	curved	thin
rectangular	narrow	rough	big
straight	heavy	short	light
wide	thick	triangular	soft
long	small	smooth	square

Adjectives A1

Adjectives A2

Adjectives B1

Adjectives B2

| LESSON NOTES | **Shapes (pages 22 and 23)** |

These pictures give practice with adjectives of shape.

Useful language

Notes	round square	rectangular	triangular
	A round cake	A rectangular box	A triangular sweet

Standard games and activities (see Section 3 pages 7–11)

Notes	[1]	What's on the Card?
	[2]	Line Solitaire
	[3]	Noughts and Crosses
	[6]	Kim's Game
	[4]	Three in a Row
	[8]	Charades
	[11]	Matching Pairs

In each game, the shape of the object must be given with the noun.

Additional activities

Odd one out

Cut out the pictures and stick them onto card to create rows of four pictures, in which three items are one shape, and one is another shape.

Happy families

Collect the different shapes of the same item, or the same shape of different items to make families.

Shapes

| LESSON NOTES | # Patterns (pages 24 and 25) |

Useful language

Notes	

T-shirts   shorts   socks   skirts   shirts
patterned   striped   plain   spotted   checked
flowered   geometric
A plain skirt   A spotted shirt

Additional language

Notes	

horizontal stripes
vertical stripes
tartan
diamond shaped pattern
blobs
triangles

Standard games and activities (see Section 3 pages 7–11)

Notes	

[1]   What's on the Card?
[2]   Line Solitaire
[3]   Noughts and Crosses
[6]   Kim's Game
[9]   Snap
[11] Matching Pairs

In each game, the pattern of the object must be given with the noun.
[12] I Went to Market
      ... and bought a striped T-shirt, a patterned skirt, some plain socks ...

Additional activities

Notes	

Odd one out

Use the blank master to create pictures:
These three shirts are plain, and this one's flowered.

Patterns

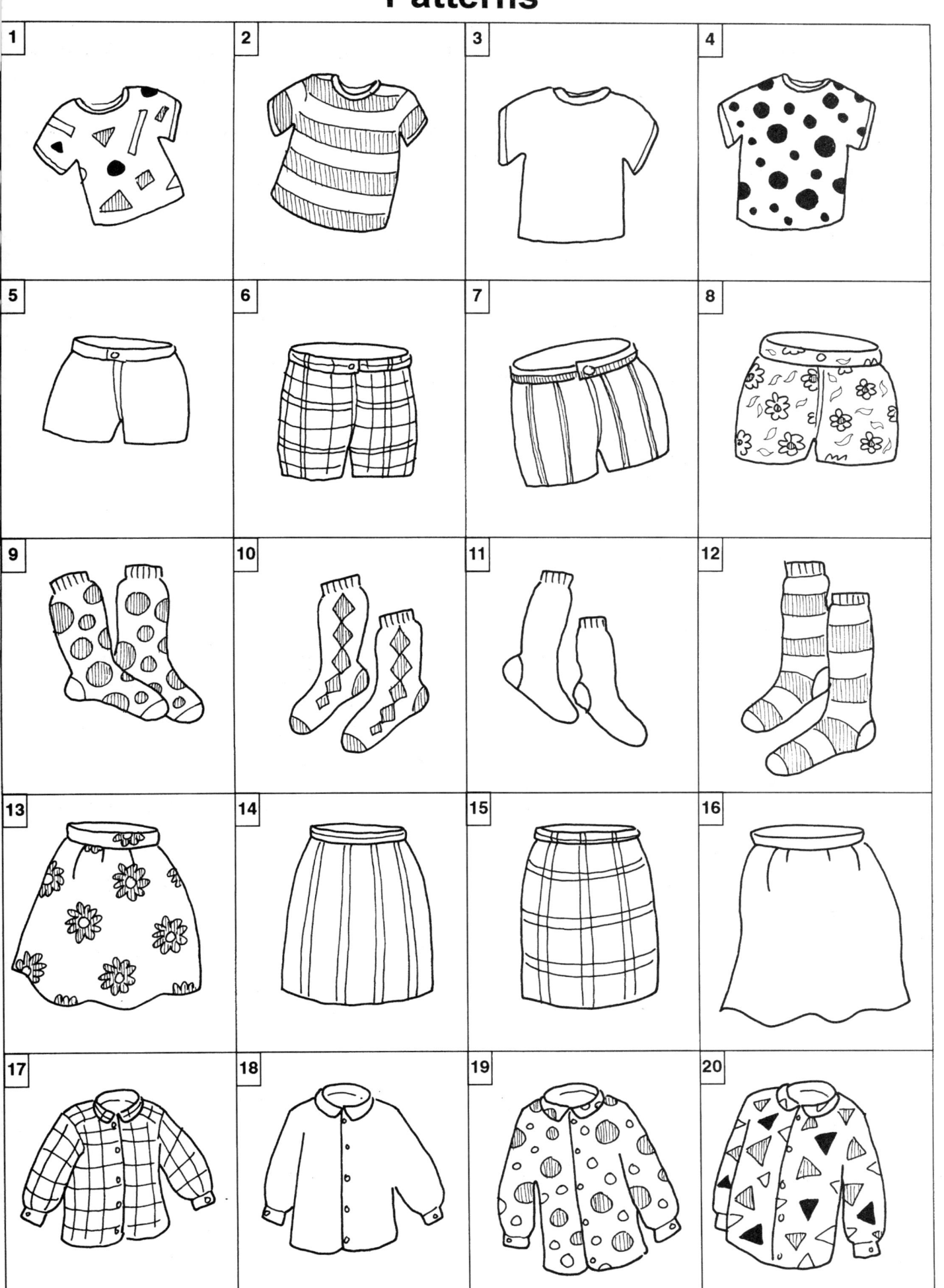

25

| LESSON NOTES | # Happy Families (1) (pages 26 and 27) |

Useful language

Notes

a checked shirt
(a pair of) striped socks
(a pair of) plain shorts

a flowered skirt
a spotted T-shirt

Standard games and activities (see Section 3 pages 7–11)

Notes

[1] What's on the Card?
[3] Noughts and Crosses
[4] Three in a Row
[11] Matching Pairs
[14] True or False?

Additional activities

Notes

Happy families

Play in groups of four. Shuffle the cards. Deal four cards to each player, and put the rest in the middle of the table, face down. The aim is to collect four cards of the same type (family). Take it in turns to ask another player:

A: Have you got a (checked shirt)?
B: Yes, I have. Here it is.

(Gives the card to A. A discards one card onto the pile.)
or

No, sorry, I haven't.

(A takes a card from the pile and discards it if it is not useful, or another card.)

The first player to get a full set calls 'Happy Family'. The player with most families at the end is the winner.

Use the blank master to make more sets of families.

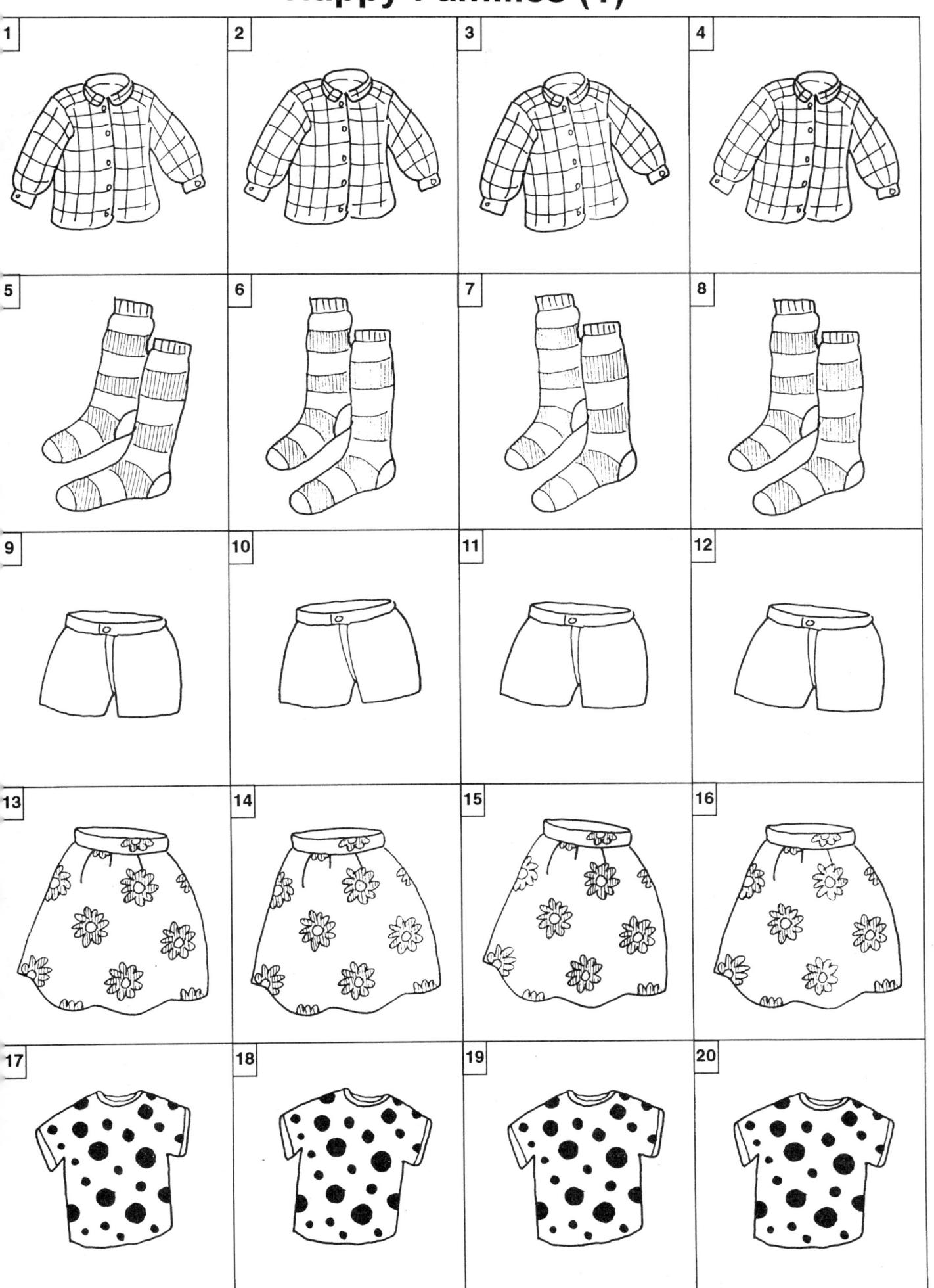

Happy Families (1)

27

| LESSON NOTES | # Happy Families (2) (pages 28 and 29) |

Useful language

Notes	a thin dog a tiny mouse a fat hen
	a small cat an enormous bear

Standard games and activities (see Section 3 pages 7–11)

Notes	[1] What's on the Card?
	[3] Noughts and Crosses
	[4] Three in a Row
	[11] Matching Pairs
	[14] True or False?

Additional activities

Happy families

Make several sets of the cards.

Play in groups of four. Shuffle the cards. Deal four cards to each player, and put the rest in the middle of the table, face down. The aim is to collect four cards of the same type (family). Take it in turns to ask another player.

    A: Have you got a (thin dog)?
    B: Yes, I have. Here it is.

(Gives the card to A. A discards one card onto the pile.)
or

    No, sorry, I haven't.

(A takes a card from the pile and discards it if it is not useful, or another card.)

The first player to get a full set calls 'Happy Family'. The player with most families at the end is the winner.

Use the blank master to make more sets of families.

Happy Families (2)

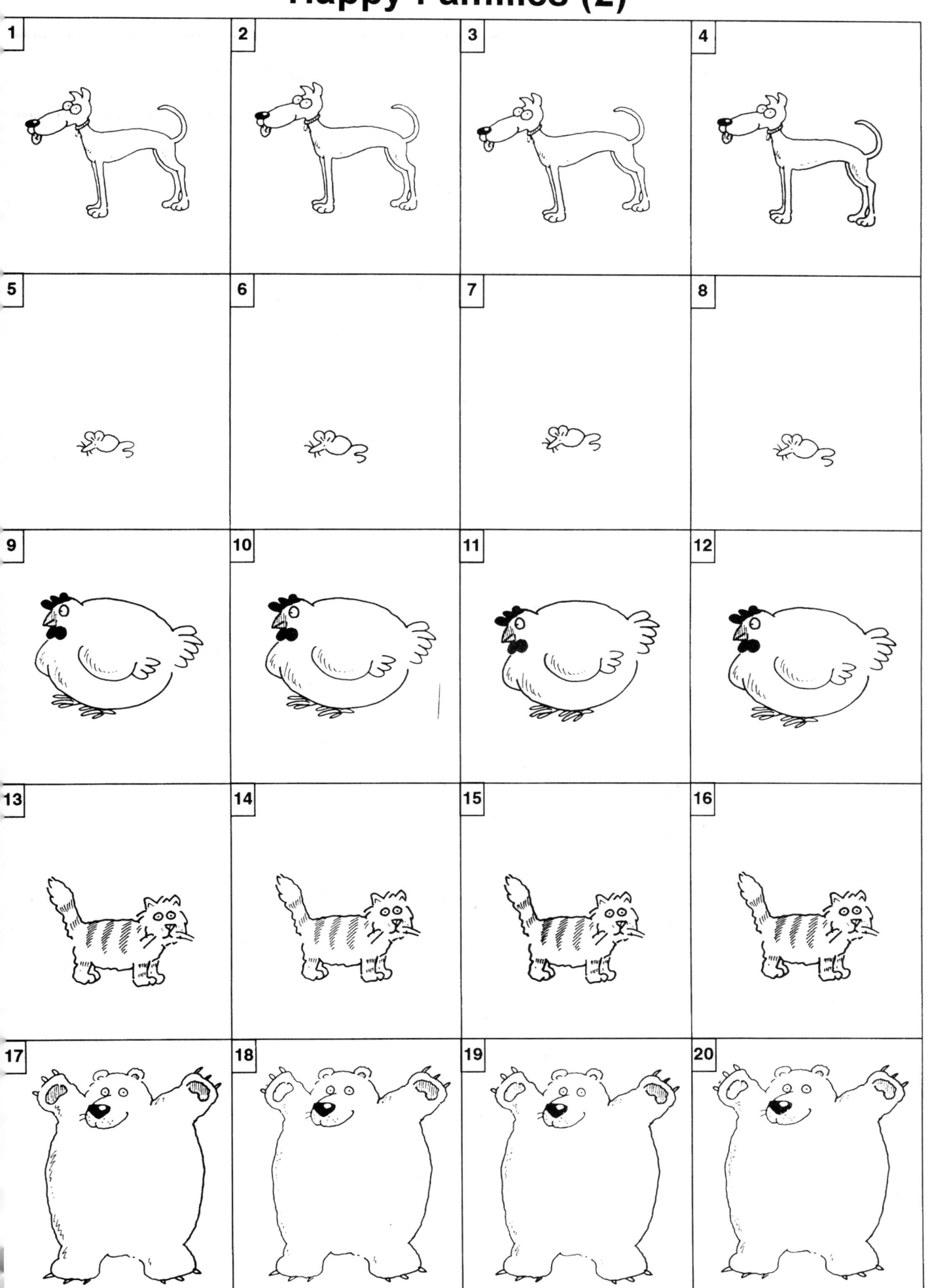

29

| LESSON NOTES | **Odd One Out (Materials) (pages 30 and 31)** |

Useful language

Notes		
	1 (made of) glass	11 (made of) metal/steel
	2 (made of) glass	12 (made of) metal/steel
	3 made of wood/wooden	13 easy
	4 (made of) glass	14 easy
	5 made of wood/wooden	15 easy
	6 made of wood/wooden	16 difficult
	7 (made of) glass	17 wet
	8 made of wood/wooden	18 wet
	9 (made of) paper	19 wet
	10 (made of) metal/steel	20 dry

Additional language

Notes
a wooden chair   a metal spoon   an easy sum
Note: substitute *plastic* for *metal* and *card* for *paper* if necessary.

Standard games and activities (see Section 3 pages 7–11)

Notes		
	[1]	What's on the Card?
	[2]	Line Solitaire
	[3]	Noughts and Crosses
	[4]	Three in a Row
	[6]	Kim's Game
	[8]	Charades
	[11]	Matching Pairs
	[12]	I Went to Market
		On the board I can see a wooden chair, a metal knife, a glass bottle ...
	[14]	True or False?

Additional activities

Happy families

Make several sets of the cards.

Play in groups of four. Shuffle the cards. Deal four cards to each player, and put the rest in the middle of the table, face down. The aim is to collect four cards of the same type (family). Take it in turns to ask another player:

A: Have you got a (wooden chair)?
B: Yes, I have. Here it is.

(Gives the card to A. A discards one card onto the pile.)
or

   No, sorry, I haven't.

(A takes a card from the pile and discards it if it is not useful, or another card.)

The first player to get a full set calls 'Happy Family'. The player with most families at the end is the winner.

Use the blank master to make more sets of families.

Materials

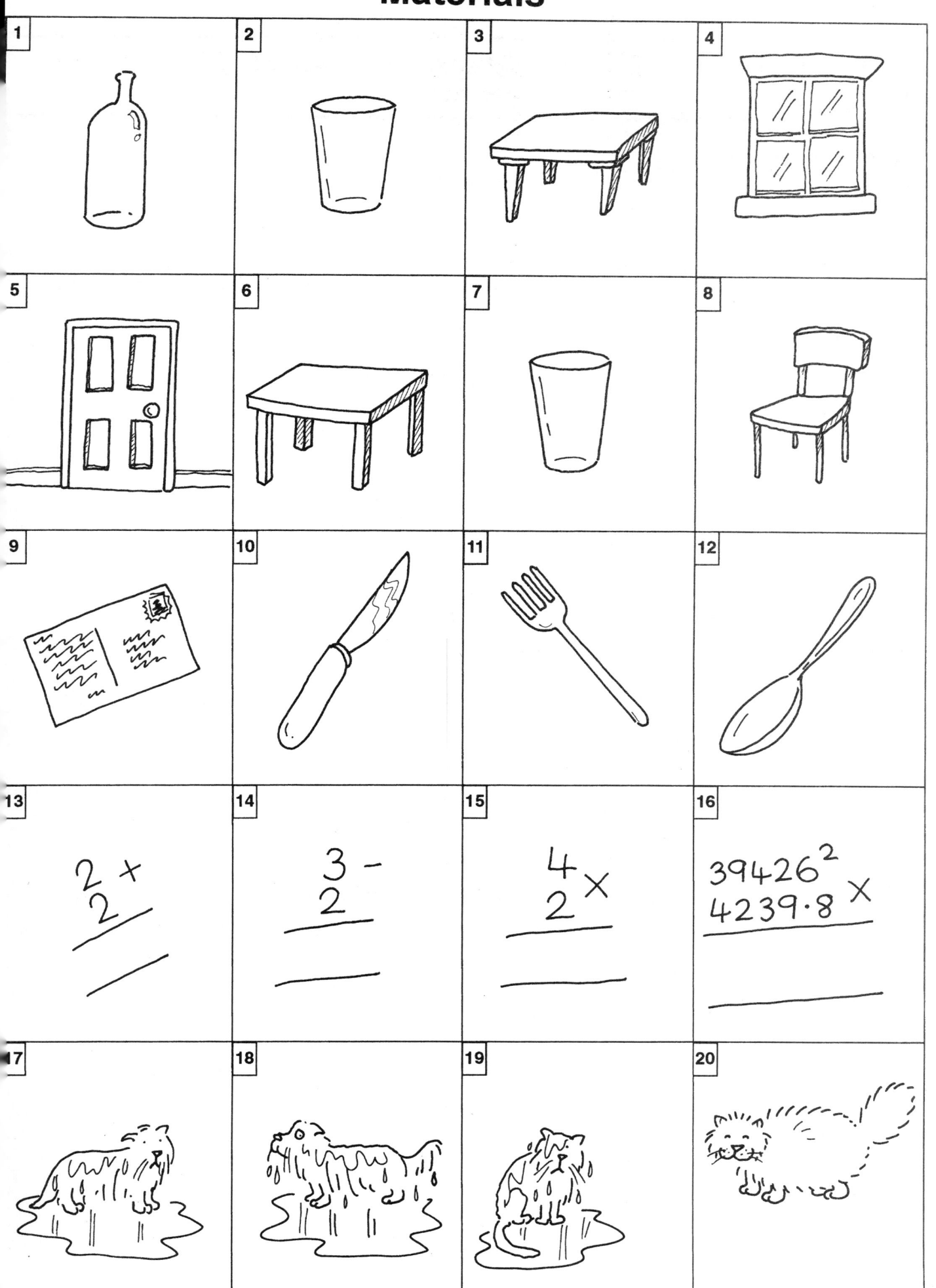

1	2	3	4
5	6	7	8
9	10	11	12
13 $\begin{array}{r}2+\\2\\\hline\end{array}$	14 $\begin{array}{r}3-\\2\\\hline\end{array}$	15 $\begin{array}{r}4\times\\2\\\hline\end{array}$	16 $\begin{array}{r}39426^2\\4239.8\times\\\hline\end{array}$
17	18	19	20

| LESSON NOTES | **Twelve Bottles (pages 32 and 33)** |

Useful language

Notes		
	1 full	7 soft/made of plastic
	2 empty	8 small/tiny
	3 broken	9 large/enormous
	4 nice/delicious	10 old
	5 nasty/horrible	11 cheap
	6 expensive	12 hard/unbreakable/made of glass

Standard games and activities (see Section 3 pages 7–11)

Notes

[1] What's on the Card?
[2] Line Solitaire
[3] Noughts and Crosses
[4] Three in a Row
[6] Kim's Game
[8] Charades
[11] Matching Pairs
[12] I Went to Market
On the board I can see an old bottle, a soft bottle, a bottle of delicious champagne ...
[14] True or False?

Additional activities

Notes

Happy families

Make several sets of the cards.

Play in groups of four. Shuffle the cards. Deal four cards to each player, and put the rest in the middle of the table, face down. The aim is to collect four cards of the same type (family). Take it in turns to ask another player:

A: Have you got (an enormous bottle)?
B: Yes, I have. Here it is.

(Gives the card to A. A discards one card onto the pile.)
or

No, sorry, I haven't.

(A takes a card from the pile and discards it if it is not useful, or another card.)

The first player to get a full set calls 'Happy Family'. The player with most families at the end is the winner.

Use the blank master to make more sets of families.

Bottles

| LESSON NOTES | # Big, Bigger, Biggest (pages 34 and 35) |

Useful language

Notes

dogs	*pullovers*	*skirts*	*parcels*	*buildings*
tiny	cheap	short	light	low
small	reasonably priced	medium-length	heavy	high
medium	dear	knee-length		
big	expensive	calf-length		
large		ankle-length		
enormous		long		

+ comparatives/superlatives of all these

Standard games and activities (see Section 3 pages 7–11)

Notes

[1] What's on the Card?
[2] Line Solitaire
[3] Noughts and Crosses
[4] Three in a Row
[8] Charades
[11] Matching Pairs
[13] Guessing Game
This dog is bigger than number 2, but smaller than number 4. (3)
[14] True or False?

Big, Bigger, Biggest

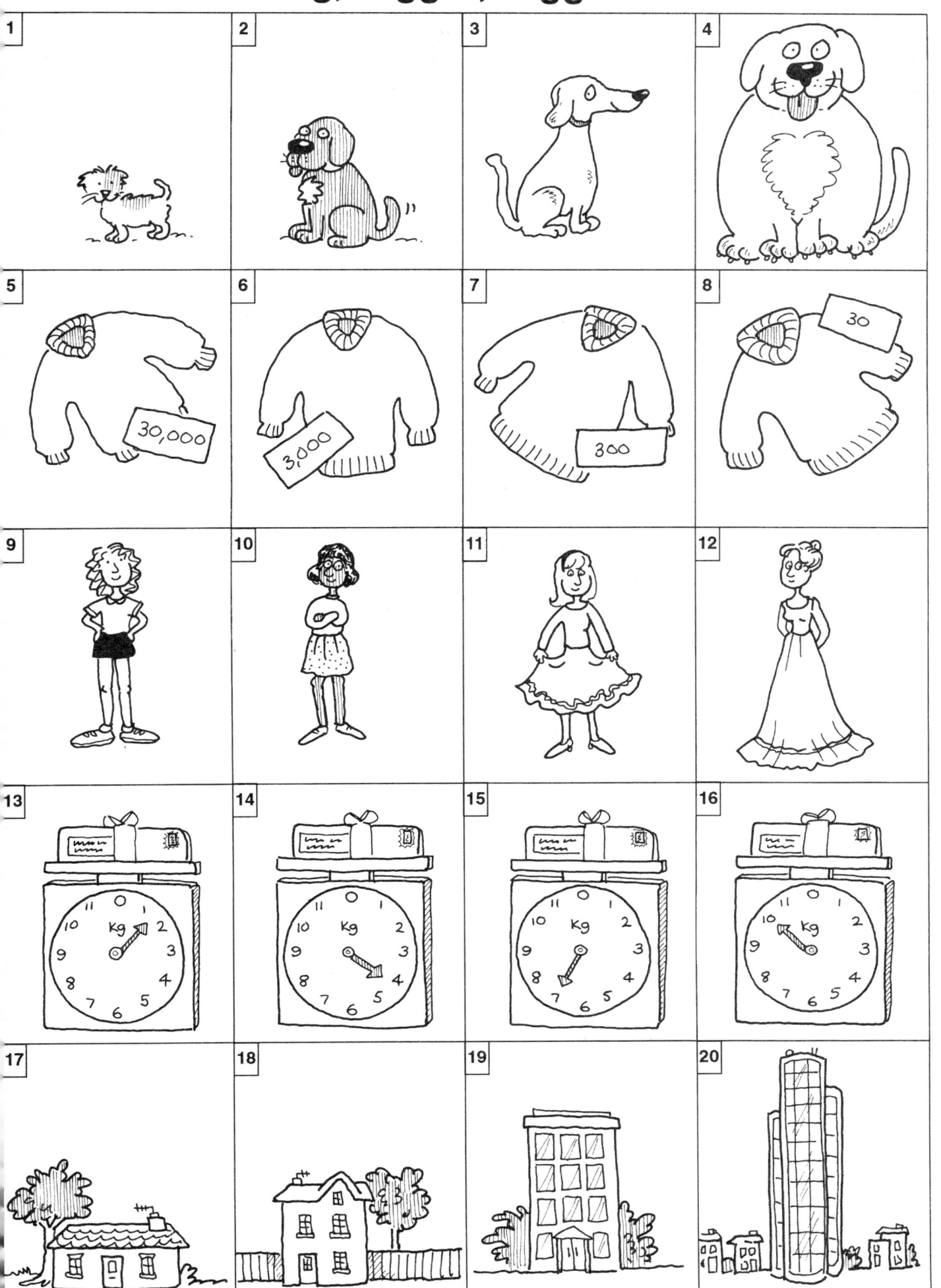

35

| LESSON NOTES | **It's too ... (pages 36 and 37)** |

These pictures give practice with modifiers and intensifiers.

Useful language

Notes		
	1 too big/long	7 too loud
	2 too small/short/tight	8 too wide
	3 too big/long	9 too hot
	4 too small/short	10 too cold
	5 too narrow	11 too high
	6 too heavy	12 too low

Additional language

Notes

much too (big)   far too (big)   not (big) enough   quite (big)

Standard games and activities (see Section 3 pages 7–11)

Notes		
	[1]	What's on the Card?
	[2]	Line Solitaire
	[3]	Noughts and Crosses
	[8]	Charades
	[11]	Matching Pairs
	[14]	True or False?

36

It's too...

| LESSON NOTES | # General Objects (pages 38 and 39) |

These pictures of common nouns are designed to be used with adjectives.

Useful language

| Notes | The chocolate is nice.
The raincoat is wet.
Nice chocolate.
A wet raincoat. |

Standard games and activities (see Section 3 pages 7–11)

| Notes | [1] What's on the Card?
[2] Line Solitaire
[3] Noughts and Crosses
[4] Three in a Row
     Take an adjective card and find a noun it could describe.
          expensive: house/car/radio
[6] Kim's Game
[11] Matching Pairs
[14] True or False? |

Additional activities

| Notes | ### Connections
Move across the board by comparing two items.
   The scarf is longer than the postcard.   *The postcard is cheaper than the car.*
   The car is dirtier than the cup.   *The tea in the cup is wetter than the foot ...* |

General Objects

| LESSON NOTES | **Two Bedrooms (pages 40 and 41)** |

The items in the pictures can be combined with adjectives. The two pictures can be used for making comparisons.

Useful language

Notes

comfortable/uncomfortable
clean/dirty
long/short
wet/dry
tidy/untidy
cheap/expensive
safe/dangerous

soft/hard
new/old
wide/narrow
small/large
quiet/noisy
warm/cold
nice/nasty

Additional language

Notes

This bed is hard, but that one is soft.
The bed in the top picture is softer than the one in the bottom picture.

How was your trip?
Great: the room was clean, the bed was comfortable, the view was lovely.
Awful: the tent was old, the bed was narrow and hard, the blankets were wet.

Standard games and activities (see Section 3 pages 7–11)

Notes

[1] What's on the Card?
    Take an adjective card and match it to one of the items in the pictures.
[13] Guessing Game
[14] True or False?
[17] Spot the Difference

Additional activities

Notes

Dream homes

Bring in pictures of rooms to compare and describe.
Describe ideal (or horror) rooms to a partner.

Two Bedrooms

| LESSON NOTES | # How was your Holiday? (pages 42 and 43) |

The items in the pictures can be combined with adjectives.

Useful language

Notes

comfortable/uncomfortable
clean/dirty
long/short
wet/dry
tidy/untidy
cheap/expensive
safe/dangerous
beautiful/ugly

soft/hard
new/old
wide/narrow
small/large
quiet/noisy
warm/cold
nice/nasty
wonderful/terrible

Additional language

Notes

How are you enjoying your holiday?
How was your holiday?

What's the hotel/pool/view like?
I hope the food will be good and ...

modern   old fashioned
broken   out of order

Standard games and activities (see Section 3 pages 7–11)

Notes

[4]   Three in a Row
      Take an adjective card and find an item it could describe.
[13] Guessing Game
      This is awful!   (food)

Additional activities

Notes

The Holiday Programme

One person comments on the pictures for a TV Holiday Programme. The rest of the group decide how many points out of ten the presenter will give to that holiday.

Use holiday brochure pictures to write about holidays, write postcards, and write letters of complaint.

Do a survey of 'holidays that went wrong'.

How Was Your Holiday ?

44

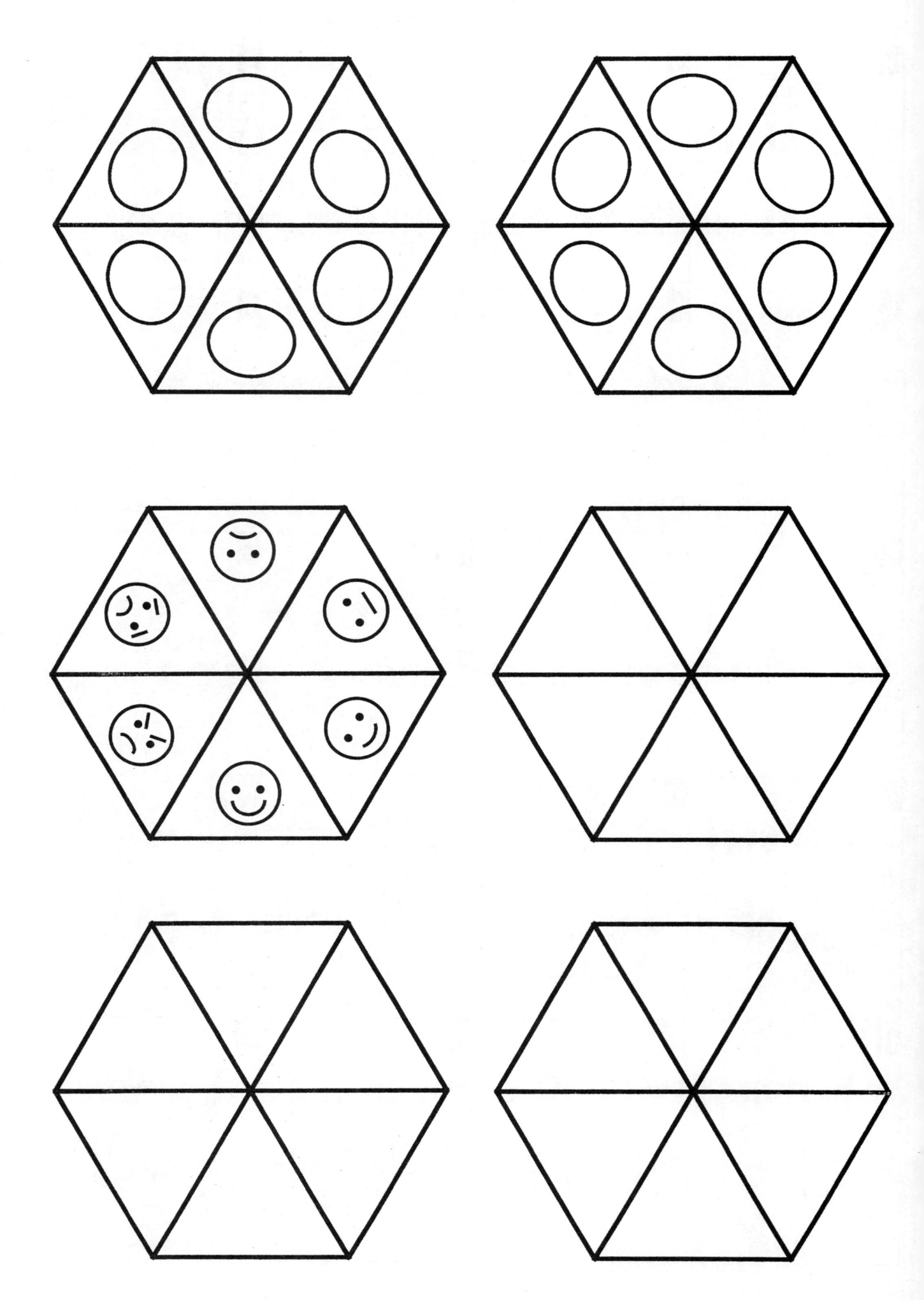

45

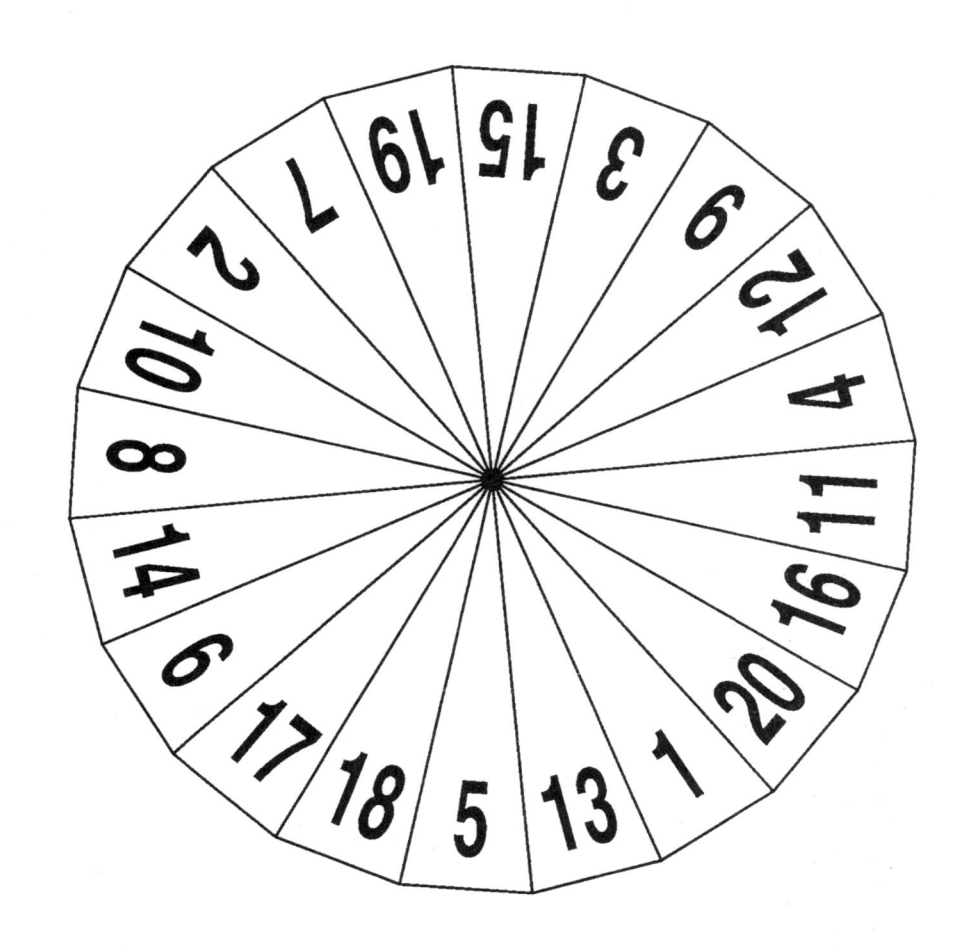

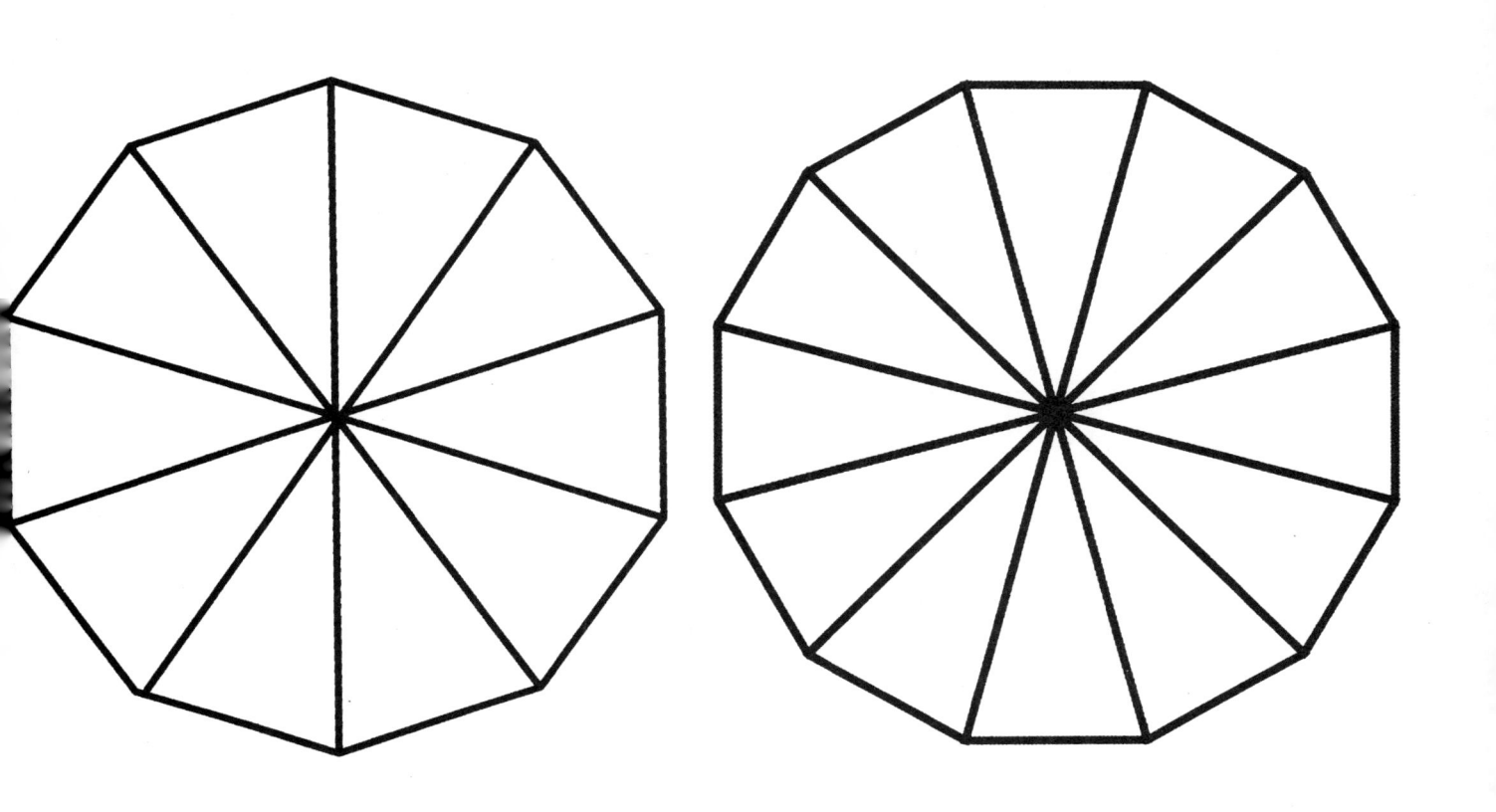

Language Chart

Page	Title	Useful Language
13	Adjectives and Opposites	*hot/cold; new/old* Comparatives and superlatives
17	Adjectives on their own	Describing objects
22	Shapes	*It's (round).* *The table is (square).*
24	Patterns	Adjective + noun Describing clothes
26	Happy families (1)	*Have you got a (checked shirt)?*
28	Happy families (2)	*Have you got a (thin dog)?*
30	Odd one out: materials	*I can see a (wooden) chair.*
32	Twelve bottles	Adjective + noun
34	Big, bigger, biggest	Comparatives and superlatives
36	It's too ...	*It's (much) too (big).* *It's not (big) enough.*
38	General objects	Matching adjectives + nouns
40	Two bedrooms	Comparing rooms *The hotel room is more comfortable than the tent.*
42	How was your holiday?	Describing and comparing holidays *It was (awful)!*